Reconnection

Emilia Alvarez Chaves

BookLeaf Publishing
India | USA | UK

Presentation by *BookLeaf Publishing*

Web: www.bookleafpub.com

E-mail: info@bookleafpub.com

ISBN: 9789357448543

First edition 2022

To my younger self, I love and forgive you

ACKNOWLEDGEMENT

To all the people that have inspired my writing, and all that have played a part in my life's story - I thank you all for loving me in your own capacities, and for however long you have.

Nothing is possible without the love and support of my family and friends. I'll never forget that. My backbone. My world.

Your Waters

Place me out in the middle of the ocean
Take me away from all that hurts me
Let me float in your waters
Submerge me in your everything
Surrounded by you, only you

Take me to your shores
Help me escape
Help me leave myself,
Back where everyone wants that person

Please want me
Take the real me with you
Let's leave them all and just be
You and me
Somewhere where expectations don't exist
Where judgement goes to die,
With no complexities or pride -
A place where love can be shared freely for both
of us

Take me to your heart

Solace

Sit close enough for you to find comfort in my
heart
Find solace in my presence
Peace in my embrace
Love in my eyes
Let me give you a moment of grace
To set you free from all that you despise

To Make a Home in My Heart

I've rearranged my furniture
And put all my pride aside
To make sure you find a place here
And hopefully mine, right beside

I don't know what I'd do
If you were to ever go
If you don't call this place home,

Because you've altered the feelings in my heart
And changed my thoughts and old habits
Coming together after being so far apart -
I freed a hook to hang your jacket.

I hope you choose to stay
Because once you're gone,
I couldn't bear with the empty space

XO

The time and space is hard
Every living, breathing thing around me that's
not you, spites me
And everything that's yours, spites me more

I used to think distance was something I needed
in order to love you
Now distance is all I have
And it kills me that I love you

The only kiss you receive from me now,
Are at the bottom of our love letters

Another Time

Because the sun will hit her eyes
And then I'm back again
It masks the distance that I felt in them

And I stay mesmerised
By the way she tells her lies
Because they make me fall another time

False God

And I was unprepared
Being your friend meant facilitating a lot less
love than what I held for you
All of a sudden I had this excess that would find
a home in all the wrong places

My heart bursting
My head filled with your image
My stomach with anxiety
My world stopped and started with you

And you didn't let me give you any of it
Now I'm suffering with potential
With all of me capable of loving you

But you made sure my love had nowhere to go
You deflected my heart
And left me in the air

My false god who knew her power

Your Waters Pt. 2

Mysterious as the ocean
You shift the tide that changes with your weather
You hit the shore
And come back different than before -
The only consistency being my disappointment,
and my longing for the one I once adored.
That each time returned with less strength;
Your waters not reaching the same lengths

You contract and relax
Moving in, while already working on moving
back out

And much like the horizon, you stay at a
distance
I won't fight against the resistance -
to get to you,
Because I thought I missed us
Or missed you

And when I inevitably get pulled into you, I
drown

Your hesitance
Your negligence

I suffocate in the relentless bashing of your
waves
One after the other, always more unpredictable
than the next
You mask all my escape routes
And make me lose sight of my firm ground, all
to make me stay

You leave me breathless
But never in the blissful, thrilling way I want to
be
Just defenceless, and helpless, wishing to be
freed

But you'll keep hitting my shore
And I'll stupidly come running back for more
Because I can't seem to part
With my masochistic heart -

But I'll never drown in you again
Never gasp for air in your presence
Never lose my balance on your painful lessons

To me you turned as dark as the oil that pollutes
you,
Not letting an ounce of light get through

So before your darkness can turn me black
I know now to swim back

The Deep End

I tried to be your helping hand
But you grasped and pulled me in
Only to find once inside, there's no safe place to
land -

And this is where it all begins

Keeping us stranded in your absence of light
You reject the sun because she's too bright
So you smother her with your dark clouded
mind
Using all her energy in this space, confined

And it's not enough to be kind
When you keep us in a bind
And blind
To all the goods things in this life

There are times where I wish to end it all
So I don't have to continue to fall
Into everything that's you
In a constant shade of blue

One day I'll escape and be free from all you do
Free from all these feelings that throw me into
the deep end of the pool

Dark Skies

The sky is always dark above me now
You took away my days
And gave me the lonely nights

The stars have no meaning
And the moon is dull

Left with no reason, only doubt
My crying eyes seem to save the drought.
All I have is the thought of you now
And the scars on my heart that show you were
felt

You were real and ever-clear
But you're not with me now -
You're not here

All My Complexities

And maybe my words didn't mean much to you
But they were all I had
You could tear them up and throw them away
But I kept writing more to make you stay.
There was so much I couldn't say,
Still coming to terms with the fact that I was gay

And I guess that's why
I couldn't love you right.
You and I,
Were never meant to comply

Maybe we were always meant to divide
To let this thing between us die -
Let the feeling go, move on with our lives

But I hope you're okay
That your life's a little less grey
Even if it lead you astray
And away -

From me, and all my complexities

Sun & Moon

The sun rose again today
Her constant reminder that the darkness never
lasts long
Even on the days I want to stray and not be okay
She's that will inside me to stay strong

My moon and her mysterious existence
She also comes to me with persistence
She's a bright light in the middle of the night
Begging me not to give up this fight

There through the storms and all the bad weather
We make it through together
Even when my mind flirts with the knife
They stay as staples in my life

And though the sun has her clouds
The moon, her black veil
Somehow the stars still shine proud
And their warming rays prevail

Our Final Division

I've been floating around my whole life hoping
to land somewhere solid
But I could never do that staying in your orbit

You made me fight myself
And I don't want this internal battle
I want to focus on my health
And not on what keeps me shackled

My life has been this one big flight
And one big fight
But I'm ready now to surrender -
It's a war I'm finally seeing the end of

I won't let others blur my vision
Or make me second guess my intuition
Keep me from making my own decisions
Or live according to their conditions

And I'll make sure I cut with precision
Our clear divide - our final division

and Forget

I forgive you
I forgive the circumstance
I forgive our immaturity
I want you to live a life rooted in positivity
And don't rob yourself the opportunity,
To find within, the precious love you deny
yourself
Stop torturing your heart from being withheld
Don't limit the wonderful woman I know you
can become
And bask in the love that I had the privilege to
learn from

Know you'll forever stay in my heart
But not in my life
I'll be wishing you well from afar
But I'll say goodbye,

Even though I don't like what that implies

Unchained

Of a veil of hate
Once too hard to placate
I've let go of the grudge
Under your tender touch

A place you'd once find
A concrete heart and mind
You helped me to unwind
From the things that kept me blind

I soften at the thought of you
And there's not a minute I'm not grateful
Because you colour in and around,
My harsh black and white bounds

I no longer care to hold the reigns -
That kept me chained
Under my false guise of control;
The torturing of my soul

I know now that love is not my pain
And I can't shrug off the blame
Letting my heart harden
Only lead to my own martyrdom

Joy

Joy
Unbridled, unapologetic, unrelenting
Come forth to me
Let me wrap you in my arms
And hold you gently in my heart

Hurricane

Not quite a storm
Or blizzard
Or even heatwave

More like a hurricane that floods my floors
Sweeps me off my feet
And drowns me;
All encompassing and disorienting

But I guess you'd call it a crush
Far too oversimplified but I guess it'll have to do -
And it's all I can do
To try and stop myself from reaching out
Because I don't know if you will grasp me.

You look really pretty from the sidelines
After all, it's a sight I've become familiar with

As well as the feeling of my hands around your
waist
And that hesitant look in your eyes that I just
can't place -
Who knows if you feel the same
Or if it's all a fantasy I've created in my brain

I don't think I can afford to think of you again,
but it won't stop.

Someone Someday

I won't resist my change
I won't hold onto pain

I'm tired of being stalled
In my fears, that would keep me enthralled

I want to love freely
From a place deeper than my trauma
To be able to show myself completely
Without space to be unsure of

I want to be good for myself
And I want to give that good self to others
To share all my wealth
To confide in a lover

I know, in my heart there's a lovely place
That will make a home for someone someday

And when that day comes
I'll know better than to try to outrun,
the hard feelings I'm presented with
Because it'll give me much more than the
resentment brings

My Potential is Great

I'm different now
I'm growing
And it's showing

And as much as I love you
It's time for me to make my way
Away -
From everything that I once knew

Staying here would be wrong
I can't be held by foundations that aren't strong

You can't tell a tree to stop growing
Or the sun that's shining to not show it
Too many people have tried to cut me down
Or cover me with their dark clouds

But I won't shroud

I know my potential is great
And I will fight to ground my heavy roots
And stretch my warming light

I'll do it through my faith
Show you what I can do
Make something of my life

My White Flag

I minimised my true heart,
In hopes of one day receiving
A wretched acceptance I so sought
But all it did was keep me bleeding

And it seemed fine at the time
Because what was one more suppressed emotion
of mine,
Already compartmentalised in a repressed part
of my mind

What was one more tear
Or one more fear -
That no one would like me
That no one could love me

I'm tired of living behind these walls
Armed and ready for a tragedy that may never
befall

I no longer wish to walk around with a loaded
gun
Or hide in my shadow, when I can stand in my
sun

So I'll surrender,
Because although it is gruelling
To resist any more of myself would be foolish

Reconnection

For too long I've been distracted by what others
think of me
And attached my meaning to the image they
painted of me

It all kept me busy.
Kept me from myself,
And fuelled the mask I wore to appease everyone -
To please anyone

I lost myself to others
And all my almost lovers

I've suffered the consequences of my
imperfections
And been bound to life's subtle misdirections -

But now it's time I face my reconnection

Back in My Body

After having been to the depths of my personal
hell
Now the sun shines through the windows of my
heart
I know that I am someone who is imperfect but
perfectly themselves
And no one can pull my self love apart

I stand strong in will
And rich in value
I sit in my peace, still
Filled with gratitude

I've finally been returned to myself
After searching far and wide for my happy
I've found my true wealth,
In the fact that no one else can do that better
than me

I've learnt to press flowers in between my pages
Bound to the work of making life more beautiful
Flowing freely through my changes
My self worth, the only thing that is immovable

Surrendering to the uncertainty of life
Surrendering to the imperfect

I surrender to my life's design
Surrendered to the feelings that have surfaced

Reconnecting to what is mine
I've found me,
After all this time.